Armor of God

The Protected Christian

Robert Frazier

Armor of God
The Protected Christian
by Robert Frazier

Printed in the United States of America

ISBN 9781613792186

Scripture quotations taken from the King James Version (KJV) – *public domain*

Cover design by Dempsey Mills

Library of Congress Cataloging-in-Publication Data
Armor of God – The Protected Christian
Religion
Christian Life
Spiritual Warfare
Body, Mind and Spirit
Inspiration and Personal Growth

www.xulonpress.com

To

All who are learning to stand "strong in the Lord and in the power of His might," putting on the Armor of God.

CONTENTS

ACKNOWLEDGEMENT

To

Paul Tharp,

whose capacity to grasp the intention of this study book
rightly enhanced the thoughts of the author.

INTRODUCTION

Armor of God

This book is intended to prepare the Christian, especially the new believer, for spiritual warfare. A disturbing reality of the Christian experience is the high spiritual casualty rate among new Christians. Perhaps they do not fully understand or appreciate the need for the protective Armor God has provided. The Apostle Paul writes in Ephesians 6:10-17:

> Finally, my brethren, be strong in the Lord and in the power of His might. Put on the whole armor of God that you may be able to stand against the wiles of the devil. For we do not wrestle against flesh and blood, but against principalities, against powers, against the rulers of the darkness of this age, against spiritual hosts of wickedness in the heavenly places.

Therefore, take up the whole armor of God that you may be able to withstand in the evil day, and having done all, to stand. Stand therefore, having girded your waist with truth, having put on the breastplate of righteousness, and having shod your feet with the preparation of the gospel of peace; above all, taking the shield of faith with which you will be able to quench all the fiery darts of the wicked one. And take the helmet of salvation and the sword of the Spirit, which is the Word of God.

After conversion, there appears to be an interlude in which the new Christian enjoys a brief respite prior to spiritual warfare. The Apostle Peter suggests this idea in 2 Peter 1:5-8, outlining the progress of spiritual maturity, the moving from *faith* in Christ to *virtue* (moral energy or zeal), to *knowledge* and then *self-control*. Self-control primes the new Christian for the trials and tests that, navigated successfully, lead to the quality of *perseverance*. The process of moving from faith to perseverance is what I would describe as boot camp.

Unfortunately, this time of equipping is often squandered in self-indulgent spiritual experiences or in well-intentioned but misplaced attempts at evangelism. When I recommitted my life to Christ at age fifteen, I remember being swept up in a spiritual fervor and making unwise attempts to convert my three sisters. When they closed their minds to me, they closed their minds to the Gospel. It took years to overcome the damage done by my misplaced zeal. A new Christian is wise not to expend his energy on premature attempts at evangelism.

God has allowed time for spiritual boot camp. In that time, the spiritual recruit learns about the protective Armor God has provided to ensure our protection, to understand the place and significance of each piece of Armor. The Armor not only guards the new Christian against becoming a casualty, it burnishes us in the soul-winning efforts that follow conversion and recommitment.

To become a protected Christian, new and recommitted Christians must keep in mind three crucial points:

1. We are in a war, like it or not.

2. We must make a stand.

3. We can be invincible. God wants us to place ourselves in harm's way, resist the enemy and cause him to flee from us as in James 4:7. The objective is to establish

a beachhead in enemy territory and force the enemy's retreat.

We are in a War.

War is defined as a state of hostilities existing between or among nations characterized by the use of military force.[1]

Some Christians are more interested in establishing a beachfront than a beachhead. We are deceived into thinking that we exist to enjoy life, enjoy our families and lay up treasures for ourselves on earth. These things are good, and there is a place for them, but our primary purpose on the earth is to establish the Kingdom of God. The Apostle Paul writes in 2 Timothy 2:4 that "No one engaged in warfare entangles himself with the affairs of this life that he may please him who enlisted him as a soldier."

Against God's implacable foe, Satan, we must engage in spiritual warfare and fight every step of the way. This philosophy may intrude on cruise time—vacations, hobbies, etc., but we need to remember that we are in a war. The war will inevitably touch the shores of our sheltered existence. Unless and until we understand this and prepare for it, we are in no shape to oppose the devil for ourselves or others.

Prime Minister Neville Chamberlain's appeasement of Germany in the run-up to World War II proved misguided and nearly fatal to the existence of the United Kingdom. The forces of liberalism and socialism he represented eschewed confrontation. Chamberlain's replacement, Winston Churchill, declared, "I have nothing to offer but blood, toil, tears, and sweat...You ask what our policy is? I say it is to wage war – by sea, land, and air – with all our might and with all the strength God can give us: To wage war against a monstrous tyranny, never surpassed in the dark, lamentable catalogue of human crime."[2]

We Christians must develop a wartime mentality. We must become protected, effective Christians to gain ground for God. We must insist that each convert usefully spend "boot-camp" time learning to outfit the Armor of God before engaging the roaring lion and his demonic hordes.

Without the *Belt of Truth*, we are susceptible to hypocrisy.

Without the *Breastplate of Righteousness*, we make decisions based on emotions or carnal rationalism.

Without the *Shoes of Peace*, we are vulnerable to insecurity.

Without the *Shield of Faith*, we are isolated and defeated.

Without the *Helmet of Salvation*, we are inclined to insubordination.

Without the *Sword of the Spirit,* we are defenseless against false teaching.

(See "Boot Camp Priorities" in Appendix B).

We have an Adversary.

We are warned in 1 Peter 5:8-9, "Be sober, be vigilant; because your adversary the devil walks about like a roaring lion, seeking whom he may devour. Resist him, steadfast in the faith, knowing that the same sufferings are experienced by your brotherhood in the world."

Satan's strategies are three-fold:

1. <u>Satan's first strategy is to deprive the Christian of his source.</u>

    Satan and his minions are no match for God or committed Christians, but if he can cut off our supply lines, we cannot withstand him for long.

    It is said, "An army marches on its stomach."[3] Our lifeline is the Word of God and prayer. Without these twin lines of connection, we are on our own and no match for the enemy. Learn about keeping these lines intact by studying "Fasting" in Appendix A.

The resource of fellowship with Christians cannot be underestimated, which is reinforced in 2 Corinthians 2:10, 11: "Now whom you forgive anything, I also forgive. For if indeed I have forgiven anything, I have forgiven that one for your sakes in the presence of Christ, lest Satan should take advantage of us; for we are not ignorant of his devices." The single most useful tool of Satan is to sow conflict among Christians and blind them to the need for forgiveness. Paul writes that sowing conflict is one of Satan's devices. Unless we can counter this isolating practice, we are vulnerable to being divided and conquered. Christians must stick together at all costs. The term "one another" is used fifty-eight times in the Epistles. The New Testament does not set forth an individual Christian experience apart from other Christians. The concept of church encapsulates the relationships of fellow Christians.[4]

2. <u>Satan's second strategy is to demoralize the Christian in his stand.</u>

It is easy to become discouraged while working for God. Even preachers may backslide while preaching the Word. But we are encouraged in Galatians 6:9: "And let us not grow weary while doing good, for in due season we shall reap if we do not lose heart."

Many battles are lost even before they are fought. "Overcoming Discouragement" in Appendix D is helpful to recognize and remedy this debilitating tendency.

Give God a chance to take your little and make much with it. Listless hands cannot fasten the Belt of Truth or lace the Shoes of Peace. One with a defeated attitude cannot place the Helmet of Salvation on a head hung low in despondency. Arms sapped of strength cannot lift the Shield or buckle the Breastplate in place. The Sword gathers dust on a table and is soon forgotten.

We have to wake up. We play right into the devil's hands when we allow him to dissemble the Armor. He knows that if we discover the protection available to us, his days are numbered.

Children of God, we are close to victory. We are inches from where we desire to be.

We must cinch up, shape up, tighten up, hook up, stand up and take up. Too much is at stake to just roll over and play dead before we have even started on our journey.

3. <u>The adversary's third strategy is to disable the Christian.</u>

We are handicapped when we are not wearing the Armor. The enemy probes until a weakness is discovered and exploited.

Without the Belt, our intentions may be good, but we are not ready for service.

Without the Shoes, we feel unable to walk the thorny path laid out before us.

Without a Helmet, we can become rebellious and insubordinate.

Without a Breastplate, our lives are marked by inconsistency.

Without a Shield, we are isolated and alone.

Without the Sword, we are defenseless against so-called worldly wisdom.

Years ago I was the pastor of a church in Colorado. The church was located near three military installations, so a segment of the congregation was active military. A family began attending our church just before the husband and father deployed to a remote assignment. Within a few months of his absence, his wife succumbed to temptation and engaged in an affair with a co-worker. She felt guilty and remorseful and confessed to God and her husband. He applied for and received hardship leave and returned home to reconcile with her.

The reconciliation was tearful and genuine. The marriage was saved and two small sons would continue to have both parents in their lives. The respite, however, proved short-lived. She was soon on my doorstep weeping. Her husband couldn't cope with feelings of betrayal and anger and sought to punish her for her indiscretion. Their ensuing separation lasted seven years, but eventually they were restored and lived a lifetime as a devoted couple.

The husband was a godly man but he had taken off the Breastplate of Righteousness after learning of his wife's affair. His own self-righteousness got in the way of God's work of grace. Satan seeks out any vulnerability to exploit to his advantage.

The key to becoming a protected Christian is to come to terms with the reality of spiritual warfare. To simply deny or ignore adversity will not make life easier; it will make it only more confusing. We must learn to recognize and combat Satan's attempts to separate us from each other and from God. He will try to stop us before we have started, fight us before we have burnished ourselves with Armor. We must learn to wear the Armor, or else we risk failure.

Make a Stand

The key to understanding spiritual warfare is emphasizing the word "stand." This word is used four times in the sixth chapter of the Apostle Paul's letter to the Ephesians:

1. "Put on the whole armor of God, that you may be able to stand against the wiles of the devil" (Ephesians 6:11). The phrase "stand against" is a soldier's expression, used for standing one's ground, not taking flight.[4]

2. "Therefore take up the whole armor of God, that you may be able to withstand in the evil day" (Ephesians 6:13a). The word "withstand" used in the manner in which the Apostle Paul uses it, means to stand against, resist, oppose, or "here to stand against the onslaught of the demons."[5]

3. "...and having done all, to stand." (Ephesians 6:13b). The verb, "stand," used with the previous word, "withstand," is the aorist imperative, which refers to simple action, without consideration of time. In other words, Paul is exhorting us simply to stand, regardless of time or circumstances. Just stand.

4. "Stand therefore..." (Ephesians 6:14a). This final word is also in the aorist imperative mood and carries the sense

of command. It is as if a commanding officer issues the order, "Ten-hut!"[6]

The thrust of this passage is defensive in nature, and so invariably, when we refer to the Armor of God, we assume erroneously that each item is defensive in nature, with the exception of the Sword of the Spirit. The Sword, by virtue of its nature, is to be used offensively.

But Paul leaves no doubt as to God's intentions. All of the Armor is defensive, even the Sword of the Spirit. Chapter Six details the defensive techniques of the Sword of the Spirit, while Chapter Seven outlines offensive strategies of the believer.

For now, it will suffice to say that when we avail ourselves of God's resources for protection, we are safe from any and every attempt by the devil and his forces to destroy our faith. God has made full provision for our complete protection. See the "Defensive Chess Strategies" for the game of Chess in Appendix E.

Be Invincible
The key to becoming a victorious Christian is to become spiritually impregnable by donning each piece of God's Armor.

This is a spiritual war. In Ephesians 6:12, Paul writes: "For we do not wrestle against flesh and blood, but against principalities, against powers, against the rulers of the darkness of this age, against spiritual hosts of wickedness in the heavenly places."

We are the Church. The Church is the Body of Christ. The Body of Christ is under attack. The devil may not be omniscient, but he is smart enough to know that his time is short. He has launched an all-out offensive against the Church, intending to destroy each and every Christian, thereby justifying his own disobedience before God. Every weapon at his disposal is being thrown at us.

Paul writes in Ephesians 4:12 the following:

Principalities: The Greek term "arche" means "the first ones," the "Arch Demons."[7] These are the evil counterparts to God's archangels. They control the movements of lesser demons.

Powers: The Greek term is "exousia" and refers to those in power. "Exousia" denotes the executive power while arche, rule, represents the authority granting the power.[8] Paul writes in Ephesians 2:2: "In which you once walked according to the course of this world, according to the prince of the power [exousia] of the air, the spirit who now works in the sons of disobedience."

Rulers: "Kosmokrator" is a compound word derived from "Kosmos," or order, or world, and "Kratos," or power or authority. Literally, the compound term means "Rulers of this world."[9]

Hosts of wickedness: The Greek term is "Poneria," which means wicked, malicious, and mischievous .[10] The demons are arrayed against us.

Paul writes in Ephesians 4:12 that Christians are standing "...against the principalities, against the authorities, against the world rulers of this darkness, against spirit-forces of perniciousness in the heavenly places."[11]

In the face of these formidable adversaries, we need all the spiritual Armor we can use. But instinctively, we lapse into the natural way of responding to the trials of life, without our Armor. Remember, ours is a spiritual warfare against spiritual foes:

For though we walk in the flesh, we do not war according to the flesh. For the weapons of our warfare are not carnal but mighty in God for pulling down strongholds, casting down arguments and every high thing that exalts itself against the knowledge of God, bringing every thought into captivity to the obedience of Christ. (2 Corinthians 10:3-5)

The devil's intention is to deprive the Christian of his source, but we can counter the devil by donning the Armor of God and engaging him on the spiritual battlefield.

God's Armor is all the armor we need. Rest assured that the devil has no surprises that the protective Armor cannot counter. His efforts to demoralize us are deflected by our confidence in God's provision for our safety.

We need every piece of Armor. We may have a preference or familiarity with a particular piece, but even the least familiar equipment is absolutely essential to guard against the disabling intentions of the devil. Forgetting our footgear can render us vulnerable to the stones and shards of his attacks of doubt.

Conclusion

It is imperative that a new Christian learn about each piece of Armor, learn its function and learn how to utilize it in order not only to survive the devil's onslaught, but to be victorious in the epic contest between good and evil.

We must burnish ourselves with the Armor of God and place ourselves in harm's way by establishing a beachhead in the enemy's territory. From there, we can launch an offensive thrust, set the captives free and pull down enemy strongholds.

Chapter One

The Belt of Truth

"Stand therefore, having girded your waist with truth."

That the first piece of Armor listed in Ephesians 6:14 is truth, truth in the "loins," truth emanating from deep within us, is significant. "Behold, You desire truth in the inward parts," the Psalmist writes in Psalm 51:6.

Truth is "sincerity without hypocrisy." Can you imagine how much simpler life would be if everyone could be counted on to tell the truth? Our overburdened legal system would be instantly vacant. Countless hours spent trying to "get at the truth" could be used for more productive purposes. If they gave up lies, misdirections, innuendos, distortions, double-dealing, guile, little white lies and fibs, Christians could be free to deal with each other in an atmosphere of trust. The word *hypocrite* comes from a word that means "to act upon the stage."[1] A hypocrite is an actor, a pretender. The Pharisees were the great religious pretenders of their day. In Matthew 23, Jesus strips off their stage masks and exposes their hypocrisy. John exposed Judas' hypocrisy in his Gospel (John 12:6) writing: "This he said, not that he cared for the poor, but because he was a thief, and had the money box; and he used to take what was put in it."

Ananias and Sapphira misrepresented the extent of their giving to the church. God killed them on the spot (Acts 5:5-10). Paul warned Timothy that in the last days, some would be "speaking lies in hypocrisy" (1 Timothy 4:2). We must pray diligently for insight to see beneath the masks of hypocrisy and discern true motives.

The Soldier's Belt

God's remedy for hypocrisy and untruth is the Christian soldier's Belt of Truth.

The Roman soldier wore a short tunic, allowing freedom of movement without any hindrance to the legs, but it was the Jewish custom of long tunics which prompted the statement, "Gird up the loins of your mind." (1 Peter 1:13) To "gird up" the loins is to gather the ends of the long robe and tuck them into the belt, allowing for quicker movement. This is illustrated in 1 Kings 18:46 when Elijah, fresh from victory at Mt. Carmel, "girded up his loins" and outran Ahab's chariot to the city.

When Christians "gird up" the loins and tuck them into the Belt of Truth, they are able to function as unencumbered soldiers of Christ, eliminating opportunities for blackmail that untruth engenders. (See Ephesians 4:27)

With the Belt of Truth, the Christian can attain a clear conscience. Satan will always test the Armor. If there are chinks in it, Satan or his cohorts will find them.

Once when I was shopping at a chain store with my son, I bought a pair of tennis shoes, but the clerk gave me too much change. I left the store thinking, "This is the blessing of the Lord. Surely, God has laid up the wealth of the wicked for the righteous—me."

But when I looked at my son, my belt felt loose. We sat down. I looked at the ticket. The clerk had short-changed the store by five dollars. I knew what I had to do.

I asked Craig what he thought we should do. He said the honest thing was to return the money. So we walked back into the store and gave the clerk the money. It felt like I tucked the hems of my robe into my belt. Craig says he doesn't remember the event, but he remembers the lesson. He is an honest man.

I've sought to free myself from the enemy's attempts at blackmail. Battling him without the Belt of Truth, I would be a feather tossed in the breeze. With the Belt cinched round my waist, I am immovable like a great tree.

Roy Robertson, who with Dawson Trotman founded the Navigators, a Christian discipleship ministry, told a powerful story of truthfulness and hypocrisy. Robertson led the follow-up ministry to the 1990 Billy Graham Crusade in Hong Kong. That crusade saw more people hearing the Gospel at one time than at any other meeting in human history.

"On the evening of December 6, 1941," he said, "My ship, the West Virginia, was docked at Pearl Harbor. A couple of the fellows and I left the ship that night to attend a Bible study. About fifteen sailors sat in a circle on the floor. The leader asked us to recite our favorite Scripture verses. Each sailor shared a verse and said a few words about it. I'd grown up in a Christian home, had gone to church three times a week, yet I sat there terrified because I could not recall a single verse. Then I remembered one: John 3:16. I rehearsed it in my mind.

"I felt the spotlight of other sailors' eyes growing closer to me as each sailor took his turn. It was on the fellow next to me. He recited John 3:16. As he spoke its significance to him, I sat in stunned humiliation. Everyone would know within a moment or two that I could not remember even a single verse of the Bible. Later, I went to bed that night thinking, 'Robertson, you're a fake.'

"7:55 the next morning, I woke to the sound of the ship alarm blaring out an order for us to get to our battle stations. The Japanese Imperial Fleet was attacking our ship and other military installations. I raced to our machine gun emplacement, but all we had was practice ammunition. For the first fifteen minutes of a two-hour battle, we fired blanks, hoping to scare off the Japanese airplanes. As I stood there firing fake ammunition, I thought, 'Robertson, this is how your whole life has been, firing blanks for Christ.' I made up my mind as Japanese bullets rattled our ship. 'If I escape with my life, I will get serious about following Jesus.'" In that instant, Robertson left his hypocrisy behind and became an honest Christian. He cinched up his belt and readied himself for spiritual battle on the front lines for God.

Conclusion

We must not allow hypocrisy to hinder us. The devil seeks out inconsistencies to use to sow doubt in our hearts and to destroy our faith. The Bible says he is a liar; he is the father of lies. But he knows where to look inside to exploit our weakness, to blackmail us, to keep us from our destiny.

Is there unresolved dishonesty in your life?

Is your word your bond?

Have you intentionally left someone with a false impression about you?

If these questions resonate, we must consider these suggestions: Quit living a lie. Gain forgiveness, and don't give the devil any place in your life. Gather up the loose ends of your life and tuck them into the Belt of Truthfulness. Get ready for a fight. Engage the devil in spiritual warfare and win others to Christ –*"Gird up thy loins now like a man."* (Job 40:7, KJV)

HOW TO HAVE A CLEAR CONSCIENCE

A clear conscience is essential to becoming a protected Christian. 1 Peter 3:15, 16 says:

"_____

_____."

After the Jews unfairly accused Paul of wrongdoing, he referred to his conscience in defense of personal integrity. Acts 24:16 states:

"_____

_____."

Before engaging in spiritual warfare, we must "give no place to the devil" (Ephesians 4:27) by allowing him to attack us on the level of a guilty conscience.

Are you certain there are no protuberances of unrepentant sins or offenses toward God or man that the devil can grasp and use to defeat you?

Steps To Take In Gaining a Clear Conscience

1. Ask God to reveal persons you have offended. Consider those with whom you have had conflicts in the past. Psalm 139:23, 24 says:

"_____

_____

_____."

As God brings them to mind, immediately ask Him to forgive you.

2. Make a list of people you have offended (Romans 14:12, 13):

"_____

_____

_____."

Prioritize the list from worst to the least and start at the top of the list. Don't attach undue importance to lesser offenses. Tackle the most difficult issues first.

1. _____

2. _____

3. _____

4. _____

3. Prayerfully approach those you have wronged, alone, at their convenience. Ask for an appointment.

   Some conversations may be best handled over the phone. Only as a last resort should you write a letter, which may not accurately express your thoughts and may later be used against your good intentions. Conversation is important because, aside from speaking, you also need to *hear* words of forgiveness.

4. Like the Prodigal Son, carefully choose your words of reconciliation and rehearse them in advance (Luke 15:17-19, 21).

5. Clearly identify your guilt, resisting the temptation to place blame on others (Matthew 7:1-5). God does not hold you responsible for their measure of guilt, but He does require you to clear you own conscience. It should sound something like, "I was wrong in _____. God has convicted me of my sin and I need to ask you, will

you forgive me?" Be sure to identify the occasion in specific language, and wait for a response to your question.

Avoid "I'm sorry." You are both sorry it happened, but that will not relieve you of a guilty conscience or one you have offended of an offended spirit.

Do not say, *"If I've been wrong,* please forgive me." You are really communicating that you are not convinced you were wrong but if the other person thinks so, then you will be a big enough person to apologize. It reveals an unrepentant heart.

6. Ask to be forgiven, and wait for a response. Do not simply make a statement of apology. If the other person is reluctant to offer forgiveness, it may indicate insincerity on your part or that restitution may be required. Do whatever is necessary to clear your conscience and to free yourself of any issue that may compromise your faith.

1 Timothy 1:19 says:

"_____

_____."

The Belt of Truth will not cinch tight over a guilty conscience. Our minds will not rest easy while there is unconfessed sin in our lives. A disturbed conscience creates anxiety and makes the Breastplate unbearable.

When we stand firm, the devil confronts us with those we have wronged and accuses us of hypocrisy. We must not retreat in the face of his accusations, which may only be partially true.

Anticipate the "wiles of the devil" (Ephesians 6:11). Prepare for the enemy's onslaught by gaining forgiveness of those you have offended.

"_____

_____" (2 Corinthians 2:10, 11).

HOW TO "BELT ON" TRUTH

Cultivate a habit of truthfulness.
Psalm 40:11 challenges:

"_____

_____."

Walter Scott said, "O what a tangled web we weave, when first we practice to deceive." Satan loves to catch Christians in half-truths and hypocrisies. When we possess "truth in the inward parts" (Psalm 51:6), we are able to withstand the attack of Satan.

Truthfully worship and serve God.

Joshua 24:14 admonishes:

"_____

_____

_____."

These are among the last words Joshua spoke to a nation that had fought long and hard in service of truth. When truth is cinched in its place, we are ready to oppose the enemy and possess the land of plenty God has promised us.

Without this deep-down truthfulness, we are neither ready to worship God nor serve Him. We tend to worship God with unresolved "stuff" weighing on our conscience. Matthew 5:23 says:

"_____

_____

_____."

Our wholehearted service is gauged by a willingness to put aside any competing "idols" and establish God's interests as our first priority. He must rank ahead of family, pleasures and ambitions.

We "belt on" truth by cinching these Scriptures tight in our spirit. We never loosen it. Never.

Chapter Two

The Breastplate of Righteousness

N ot long ago, I met a cop and wondered if the Kevlar vest he wore made him feel hot and uncomfortable. I asked him if he ever considered not wearing one. "Yes," he said. "Some other officers don't wear them at all. But I wouldn't take it off for any reason. It's my protection."

So is the Breastplate of Righteousness the Christian's protection. The phrase *having on* means literally "put on and keep on."[1]

The phrase is used in Ephesians 6:14, 15 to refer to the *Breastplate*, to the *Belt* of Truth and to the *Shoes* of Peace.

Contrast it with the phrase, t*ake up* in verses 16 and 17, which cautions "to use as needed" the *Shield*, the *Helmet* and the *Sword*.

There isn't any right time or place to lay aside the righteous protection of the Breastplate. Righteousness is nothing without integrity. It wards off the effects of what Prince Hamlet called the slings and arrows of outrageous fortune, the excuses one makes who shuns responsibility, that darken the soul. One must wear the light of righteousness on the chest and by wearing it proclaim it. It must remain in place.

The Breastplate is pressure.

Righteousness is restrictive. Bearing the weight of the righteous Armor can be a burden. It doesn't always fit, and the folds in it can pinch and chafe. The believer seldom forgets it is on. It is an ache, a kind of slow suffering, and the world and its masters are always asking us to take it off. But it is our protection.

It covers the vital organs, at the center of which beats the human heart. In the Western mindset, the heart is the seat of emotion. Songs and literature across the ages have romanticized the heart as a fountain of gushing sentimentality.

The Bible, however, whose origin is Eastern, characterizes the *heart* as the seat of intelligence: "For as a man thinks in his heart, so is he." (Proverbs 23:7)

Mark writes in his Gospel that "For from within, out of the heart of men, proceed evil thoughts, adulteries, fornications, murders, thefts, covetousness, wickedness, deceit, lewdness, an evil eye, blasphemy, pride, foolishness. All these evil things come from within and defile a man" (Mark 7:21-23).

The heart is a reflection of our innermost thoughts. Consider the following passages from the Bible:

Psalm 14:1—"The fool has said in his heart, there is no God."

Psalm 15:2—"He who walks uprightly and works righteousness, and speaks the truth in his heart."

Psalm 45:1—"My heart is overflowing with a good theme; I recite my composition concerning the King."

Psalm 119:11—"Your Word I have hidden in my heart that I might not sin against You, O Lord."

Proverbs 2:1-5—"My son, if you receive my words, and treasure my commands within you, so that you incline your ear to wisdom, and apply your heart to understanding; yes, if you cry out for discernment, and lift up your voice for understanding; if you seek for her as silver, and search for her as for hidden treasures; then you will understand the fear of the Lord and find the knowledge of God."

Proverbs 4:23—"Keep your heart with all diligence, for out of it spring the issues of life."

Proverbs 22:17—"Incline your ear and hear the words of the wise, and apply your heart to my knowledge."

Proverbs 23:7—"For as he thinks in his heart, so is he."

Personal integrity is not only a matter of actions and words. We are not entitled to think anything we choose to think. Jesus forbade a man to look at a woman with lust, for he "has already committed adultery with her in his heart." (Matthew 5:28) Paul reminded the Corinthians that "The weapons of our warfare are not carnal but mighty in God for pulling down strongholds, casting down arguments and every high thing that exalts itself against the knowledge of God, bringing every thought into captivity to the obedience of Christ." (2 Corinthians 10:4-5) Righteousness protects us from our own unlawful imaginations.

The Breastplate covers *how we feel*. The King James Bible references "bowels" of compassion in 2 Corinthians 6:12, Philippians 1:8, 2:1, Colossians 3:12, and Philemon 7, 12 and 20. The NKJV, NASB, NIV, etc., superficially translate "bowels" as heart, as affection, tender mercies, etc. Only the King James version of the Bible captures the deep-seated emotional response in, for example, 1 John 3:17: "But whoso hath this world's goods, and seeth his brother have need, and shutteth up his bowels of compassion from him, how dwelleth the love of God in him?"

The translators, I believe, eschewing "bowels" sacrificed accuracy for delicacy. But the Breastplate covers also the bowels. Perhaps in the heat of our emotional responses to stimuli, the pressure of His righteousness is brought to bear in our hearts and our bowels.

We must resist the pressure of the enemy to free ourselves of the weight of righteousness. We embrace the weight of righteousness. We wear the burden of the Breastplate not because it is easy or comfortable, but because it is righteous. We resist the fancies of the moment, fleeting emotions, vapid expressions. The restraint of integrity checks our thoughts and screens those concepts and visages that do not edify us. "Keep your heart with all diligence, for out of it spring the issues of life." (Proverbs 4:23)

"Finally, brethren, whatever things are true, whatever... are noble, whatever...are just, whatever things are pure, whatever things are lovely, whatever things are of good report, if there is...anything praiseworthy— meditate on these things," Paul writes in Philippians 4:8. True things— noble, just, pure, lovely and praiseworthy and of a good report—are not always comfortable. The Breastplate pinches us when our thoughts stray into the forbidden places, when unchristian outbursts well in us. Our skins chafe against the Breastplate to the point of rawness. A dear sister of mine used to excuse her periodic venting, saying, "Pastor, I'm sorry, but that's the Irish in me." I said, "Sister, that's the devil in you, and it's got to stop!"

Believers are tempted to relieve the discomfort by detaching the Armor, but that is the last thing we should do. Treat the symptoms by avoiding unholy stimuli. Rub the ointment of forgiveness and grace on chafed skin. Seek not vengeance. The Christian who guards against unrighteous thoughts and feelings will avoid unrighteous deeds.

Integrity is expressed in self-control. Are your thoughts, words, and actions under the control of the Holy Spirit? A quiz on "Self-Control" is available at the end of this chapter.

We have a fallen nature. When Satan attacks us, he comes at us through our human natures. It is *natural* to allow ourselves to feel depressed, to think negative thoughts, to get upset or imagine the worst. Negativity resonates in us. It feels good to purge our system through emotional outburst or an anger-venting tirade.

Satan knows how to capitalize on our basest instincts, to lure us into unrighteous responses. It is God's Breastplate of Righteousness that comes between Satan's attack and our natural impulses toward unrighteousness.

This Armor pinches unholy thoughts and checks our propensity to sin. "Let no one say when he is tempted, 'I am tempted by God; for God cannot be tempted by evil, nor does He Himself tempt anyone. But each one is tempted *when he is drawn away by his own desires and enticed*. Then, when desire has conceived, it gives birth to sin; and sin, when it is full-grown, brings forth death." (James 1:13-15)

The Armor chafes and rubs at angry outbursts, warning us that wounds we impose on others have an effect upon us, and if untreated, can result in fatal infections to our spiritual condition. James 1:20 states, "For the wrath of man does not produce the righteousness of God."

Integrity means doing the right thing, regardless of how we feel or what we think.

Conclusion: If the Belt of Truth signifies *sincerity*, the Breastplate of Righteousness represents *integrity*. Integrity is impossible without sincerity. If we are not entirely truthful, we become an easy target for the devil's blackmailing efforts. In other words, unless the Belt is in place *all the time*, the Breastplate will not stay on. Before we can hope to manage thoughts and feelings, we must come clean before God and begin living a consistent Christian life. Anything less will result in a compromised Christian experience.

The Breastplate prepares the way for the Shoes of Peace, to stand firmly on the bedrock truth of God's Word. The next chapter on the Shoes of Peace will further solidify the Christian against the onslaught of the enemy.

SELF-CONTROL QUIZ

1. Do you have any self-destructive habits that harm your body or damage your testimony?

Romans 12:1 —

"_____

_____."

Romans 14:15 —

"_____

_____."

1 Corinthians 3:16 —

"_____

_____."

2. Do you regularly have negative or unclean thoughts that cause you to yield to temptation?

Philippians 4:8 —

" _____

_____ . "

3. Are you troubled by inappropriate emotions, such as outbursts of anger, lust, covetousness, etc.?

Mark 7:20-23 —

" _____

_____ . "

The Breastplate of Righteousness interrupts the fleshly thoughts and feelings which connect with the temptation to sin. Shape up to keep up.

HOW TO "BUCKLE UP" THE BREASTPLATE

The believer's personal righteousness or integrity is described as Armor: "Stand therefore ... having put on the breastplate of righteousness" (Ephesians 6:14).

Paul wrote in 2 Corinthians 6:7 that his personal integrity commended him to the Corinthians:

"_____

_____."

In Isaiah 59:17, the Lord searched for one who would intercede for His people and found none. So He put on Armor and did the job Himself.

"_____

_____."

The Breastplate of Righteousness protects the heart and mind. Its defensive nature allows us to stand in the face of fear and doubt. In 1 Corinthians 7:37, Paul uses the expression, *"to stand steadfast in his heart,"* to commend the resolution of a father in preserving his daughter's virginity.

49

The Breastplate of Righteousness guards against misgivings caused by worldly opinions. Others may not understand our actions, but if righteous intentions are in place like a Breastplate, we can withstand the buffeting winds of public opinion. With the Breastplate in place, we know He is right and are not swayed by others' arguments or doubts.

While 1 Corinthians 7:37 describes the Breastplate as a protection against wrong ideas, Philippians 4:1 provides that it offers protection against wrong feelings.

The Apostle's unqualified love protected him against unhealthy attention from ungodly people (Philippians 3:17-19). In the same way, a father extends righteous love toward his daughter. His love is a breastplate of protection for her against the unwholesome intentions of ungodly men.

How do we put on the Breastplate of Righteousness?

First, start each day by repudiating sin. 1 Corinthians 15:34 states,

"_____

_____." We must suppress our own thoughts of sin.

Secondly, we must quiet our emotions in an island of peace. Isaiah 32:17 reads,

"_____

_____."

When our thoughts are managed and our emotions checked through self-control, we are able to wear the Breastplate and enjoy the protection the Armor of God affords.

Chapter Three

The Shoes of Peace

The effect of cinching the Belt round the Breastplate cascades down to the Shoes. The Belt of Truth guards against hypocrisy. When we are truthful, our Breastplate of Righteousness fits snugly in place. If we manifest hypocrisy or untruth, the Breastplate becomes uncomfortable, too heavy to wear for long. The Breastplate shields our baser instincts from the enemy's coaxing and temptations, enabling us to wear the Shoes of Peace.

The Shoes of Protection

Our soldier Shoes are our standing with Christ. From them comes our capacity to stand firmly on the Word of God. His Word is a solid rock; but if we cannot stand on it, it is no good. The word *preparation* means "readiness." In Hellenistic Greek, it was used to mean establishment, firm foundation, or firm footing.[1]

Christians moving in close quarters tend to step on each other's toes. When that happens, we should get over it; but when we are not sure-footed, trifling issues mushroom into acrimony. If we are easily offended, we need to check our equipment. Are we wearing our Shoes? God expects us to close ranks with fellow believers, but our fallen nature makes it inevitable that we will be hurt and in turn hurt others. If only our Shoes were made of steel!

They are not bedroom slippers, and they are not always comfortable. Remember, this is war, and our Shoes' first value is their utility in battle. Their comfort quickly fades when we face the reality of standing firm at any cost.

The Shoes are not fashionable. God is not concerned with fashion. Style and color are irrelevant. They are designed to help us stand firm on principle. Paul wrote in 1 Corinthians 15:58, "Therefore, my beloved brethren, be steadfast, immovable, always abounding in the work of the Lord, knowing that your labor is not in vain in the Lord."

The Shoes are not for running or marching; they are for *standing*. Our soles are melded in God's Word and cannot be shaken. When storm winds buffet us, we stand firm and secure. As long as we are melded with the Word of God, we cannot be moved.

We must wear Shoes that fit. We should not attempt to wear the pastor's shoes. We should not wear our spouses' or our parents' shoes. We must stand on God's Word for ourselves.

In the Psalm 73, Asaph depicts Israel as being "pure in heart," then contrasts his own condition. "Truly God is good to Israel, to such as are *pure in heart. But as for me,* my feet had almost stumbled; my steps had nearly slipped. For I was envious of the boastful, when I saw the prosperity of the wicked." Asaph had loosened his Belt of Truth and became hypocritical and insincere. He was afflicted with an impure heart. With the Belt loosened, he could not wear the Breastplate of Righteousness. His thoughts and feelings were left unguarded. So he began to question his relationship and standing with God. Not until Verse 17 does he go "into the sanctuary of God: Then I understood their end."

In God's presence, he lays bare his own heart and realizes he isn't wearing any Armor. "Surely, You set them in slippery places," Asaph writes of being without the Belt, the Breastplate and the Shoes.

Without the Shoes, when the world moves, we move. The winds of catastrophe buffet us, but if we wear the Shoes and embrace the gospel of peace, we will stand firm. God's truth is a mountain in a storm.

Luke writes in Acts 20:24 of the Apostle Paul telling the Ephesian elders, "But none of these things *move me;* nor do I count my life dear to myself, so that I may finish my race with joy and the ministry which I received from the Lord Jesus, to testify to the gospel of the grace of God." The Belt of Truth was cinched in place; his intentions were sincere. The Breastplate of Righteousness protected him from fear and doubt. With his feet planted firmly in the Shoes of Peace, he was immoveable. He was dressed for spiritual warfare, to win God's victory.

When we wear the Armor, we are safe everywhere all the time. The tumults of our lives need not separate us from the truth of Scripture. The world has been made over a thousand-thousand times, and it may make itself a thousand-thousand times more, but the Scripture shall remain.

We need not worry about salvation. With the Belt and Breastplate in place and God's Shoes on our feet, we are as safe as we are ever going to be. No one, nothing can ever "separate us from the love of God which is in Christ Jesus our Lord." (Romans 8:39)

The Shoes of Preparation

The Shoes of Peace help us prepare to live the gospel of peace. Standing firm on the Word of God is not ministry, but doing so is a necessary precursor to ministry. Without the secure footing of the Gospel, we are easily moved "to and fro and carried about with every wind of doctrine, by the trickery of man, in the cunning craftiness of deceitful plotting." (Ephesians 4:14)

Our personal issues must be resolved if we are to engage the enemy in spiritual warfare. We cannot be at war within ourselves and yet hope to withstand the onslaught of the enemy. *Peace* is a personal, inner peace. It is nearly impossible to win a war fought on two fronts, versus the devil without and our own doubts and insecurities within.

A superficial, hypocritical Christian, riddled with self-doubt and lustful yearnings, has no hope of standing firm in tough times. With the Belt and Breastplate on and the Shoes holding fast to the rock of God's truth, we are prepared to minister. Without them, despite our honorable intentions to minister, we become as "castaways." (1 Corinthians 9:27, KJV)

When we are at peace with God and standing firm in our faith, when our word and life are melded in the bedrock principles of God's Word, we pave the way for His message. Our first ministry is the example we set of a consistent, Godly life.

Check out the Scriptural principles in the following pages to see how to stand rock-solid.

PRINCIPLES UPON WHICH TO STAND

The Christian soldiers' footgear allows us to stand firm and make way for the gospel of peace. We stand firm on slippery ground and withstand the buffeting lies of Satan. Consider some principles from Scripture that provide a solid footing.

1. Spiritual Freedom (Galatians 5:1)—

"_____

_____."

The earth trembles when we substitute the traditions of man for the salvation of grace. The Galatians were in danger of

abandoning the high ground of grace in favor of the familiarity of man's reason and traditions. "For by grace you
have been saved through faith, and that not of yourselves;
it is the gift of God, not of works lest anyone should boast."
(Ephesians 2:8-9)

2. Sound Doctrine (Ephesians 4:14)—

"_____

_____."

The bedrock of truth holds us firm admidst the swirl of false
teaching and popular man-centered "theology." The example
of the early Church helps us to "get a grip" in these uncertain
times. (Acts 2:42)—

"_____

_____."

3. Steadfast Ministry (1 Corinthians 15:58)—

"_____

_____."

We cannot allow half-hearted ministry to give us "happy
feet," looking here and there for fulfillment in life, in place

of solid ministry that paves the way for the gospel of peace to extend the Kingdom of God. (Romans 14:17)—

" _____

_____."

4. Sudden Return of Christ (2 Thessalonians 2:1-2)—

" _____

_____."

False teachers declared that Christ had already come and there was no more to anticipate from God. We stand rock-solid in the hope of His return. He will do everything He said He would do, including lifting us up on high to stand in His presence for eternity.

STAND FOR REVIEW

These pieces of Armor—the Belt, the Breastplate, and the Shoes—are to be worn at all times. The Shield of Faith, the Helmet of Salvation and the Sword of the Spirit are to be taken up as needed. To venture forth without truthfulness (the Belt of Truth), without consistent management of our thoughts and feelings (the Breastplate of Righteousness), and continuous stability (the Shoes of Peace), we risk rendering inoperable the remaining pieces of Armor. Putting on and keeping on the first three pieces of Armor is a prerequisite to taking up as needed the Shield, the Helmet, and the Sword. The first three pieces of Armor enable us to engage in spiritual self-defense. Even with the Armor, we cannot win without the grace of God. We are not spiritually self-reliant.

Nonetheless, we must be engaged in our own defense. We cannot expect God to do the heavy lifting. Paul wrote in Philippians 4:13 that "I can do all things through Christ who strengthens me." Christ strengthens us, but the lifting is our cross.

How are we to engage in our spiritual defense?

We must live "without offense toward God and men." (Acts 24:16) The enemy will confront us with inconsistencies between our profession and our walk. That is why our sins must be forgiven and our conscience clear before God. This is what it means to cinch up the Belt of Truth.

Early-on in my pastorate, at the conclusion of a church board meeting, I asked board members if there were any issues that needed to be addressed. "Pastor, at least five families in this church don't want you as their pastor," a board member said. Hurt and embarrassed, I replied, "Who are the families? What can I do to correct the problem?" "They have asked me not to mention their names," the board member said. I closed the meeting.

In the solitude of my office, I wondered if I should resign. My doubt morphed into anger. I wanted to toss them all out and start over. Fortunately, I had recently attended a seminar where attendees were instructed on "What to do when members react to your ministry." I reviewed the material and drew strength from its outline for reconciliation. Instead of focusing on how I had been wronged, God showed me how I had offended others with my attitude of pride and insensitivity. God shared the identity of those dissatisfied with me through the conviction of my own failings. I became broken in spirit and repented before the Lord with hot tears of shame.

One at a time, I made appointments with the offended families and detailed the instances in which I had failed them as pastor, begging their forgiveness. I have never been a crier, but in those meetings, I could not stop my tears. God not only allowed me to be broken, He also broke the back of insubordination brewing in our church. Since that time, I have enjoyed the measure of grace that is due those of whom James writes, in James 4:6, for "God resists the proud, but gives grace to the humble."

We must manage how we feel and what we think with the Breastplate of Righteousness. We cannot deny the pull of fleshly desires. It is unwise to discount or deny them. God's Breastplate of Righteousness provides for our defense against them, enabling us to resist them and stand firm.

We act with integrity when we do what is right, no matter what we think or how we feel.

I read in the magazine *National Racquetball* of Reuben Gonzales, a player who was in the final match of a professional racquetball tournament:

"It was Gonzales' first shot at a victory on the pro circuit, and he was playing the perennial champion. In the fourth and final game, at match point, Gonzales made a super 'kill' shot into the front wall to win it. The referee called it good. One of two linesmen affirmed that the shot was in. But Gonzales, after a moment's hesitation, turned around, shook his opponent's hand and declared that his shot had skipped into the wall, hitting the court floor first. As a result, he lost the match. He walked off the court. Everyone was stunned. The next issue of *National Racquetball* featured Reuben Gonzales on its cover. The article about him sought to explain his actions. A player with victory in hand disqualified himself on match point, and lost. When asked why he did it, Reuben said, 'It was the only thing I could do to maintain my integrity.'"[2] Reuben's Belt was cinched tight, and his Breastplate deflected the enemy's attempt to shower on him an undue victory.

Standing firm, as Reuben did, is only possible when we wear the Shoes of preparation for the gospel of peace. The gospel of peace is the inner peace of the individual Christian. Battles are seldom won against enemies when the combatant is simultaneously fighting oneself. The battles within us sap us of the energy and attention necessary to wage spiritual warfare. Riddled with self-doubt and insecurity, we question our worthiness to be soldiers in God's army. We must become secure with ourselves before we can feel secure of our place in God's cause. We must put on and leave on the peace of God. He has made us precisely as we are and has assigned to each of us a place. He has confidence in us and has provided the Shoes of personal peace to enable us to stand without wavering. "We cannot control the tragic things that happen to us, but we can control the way we face up to them."[3]

The first three pieces of the Armor of God offer inner protection:

- When the Belt of Truth is cinched tight, it guards against insecurity.
- When the Breastplate of Righteous integrity is properly fitted, it protects us from personal inconsistency.
- The Shoes of inner Peace shield us from instability.

The next three items of Armor offer protection from the assaults of Satan and are to be taken up when we are attacked.

- When the devil attacks us for inconsistencies revealed by our past actions and endeavors, we hold up our Shield of accountability.
- When Satanic hordes seek to cut us off from the protection of authority figures, we fit the Helmet of submission to authority on our heads and come under the protection of those who "watch out for your souls." (Hebrews 13:17)
- When the devil attacks us directly, we fight him with the Sword of the Word of God.

The Belt, the Breastplate and the Shoes offer inner protection.

The Shield, the Helmet and the Sword are used to combat Satan's overt assaults. Let us consider the latter three in turn.

Chapter Four

The Shield of Faith

"Above all, take the Shield of Faith with which you will be able to quench all the fiery darts of the wicked one," Paul writes in Ephesians 6:16.

The Shield protects us from flaming arrows shot from both within our circle and from afar.

Snipers take aim at our hearts from their far-off perches. But do not forget that it was his own brother, Cain, who killed Abel; that David's own son, Absalom betrayed him.

God has provided Armor designed to ensure our safety as we engage in spiritual warfare. When we wear all the pieces together, we are invincible. Some new Christians, however, launch into battle before learning to wear the Armor. They "… fall short of the grace of God." (Hebrews 12:15)

We must learn to buckle on the Belt and the Breastplate, to traverse the field of battle in the Shoes. When the flaming arrows rain down, we must take up the Shield. It must always be on hand, ready to be taken up at a moment's notice. Heed the reasoned warnings of our brethren. Trust not the impunity of our impulses when our brother's or our sister's words are wiser. Nowhere does the Bible teach a kind of "go-it-alone" spirituality in which Christians face the devil alone. The adversary seeks to isolate and alienate Christians. Confronted alone, we are more prone to accede to the sweetness of his promises. For that reason, God hates "…one who sows discord among brethren." (Proverbs 6:19).

Above All

The Apostle Paul wrote in Ephesians of the Shield being used "in addition to all."[1] The expression signals a shift in emphasis. The first three pieces of Armor were to be *put on* and *kept on*. The last three are to be *taken up*, which suggests that we tread not always at the fore on the field of battle. Even when we are alone, in a time of rest, we must not set aside our sincerity (Belt), our integrity (Breastplate) or our stability (Shoes). The Shield, the Helmet and the Sword are *taken up* in anticipation of imminent spiritual combat.

The Shield of Faith

The Roman soldier used two basic types of shields. The first resembled a large Frisbee and was worn on the forearm. It was especially useful in hand-to-hand combat, its small size and weight enabling the soldier to move it about freely. It was of little use against arrows or heavy javelins. A different shield was used to deflect those. This was one Paul described in Ephesians. "This shield was large and oblong, measuring some four feet by two-and-a-half feet."[2] The legionaries believed one should "Come back with your shield or on your shield."[3] A soldier should return from battle either with his shield, or on it—as a corpse carried by his fellows. The shield Paul described here was large enough for the latter purpose.

The Christian can deploy both shields. In fact, shields are most effective when used in tandem. The Romans practiced a defensive position in which the shields overlapped in front, on top, and along the flanks. They might have been giant turtles in their shells, and their "testudo" was the forerunner of the modern armored tank.

Linking our Shields together with other Christians' Shields endows us with a sense of responsibility and more importantly, accountability. When we stand shoulder-to-shoulder with fellow believers, Satan cannot so easily isolate and target us with "fiery darts." Seasoned as we may be, we are all vulnerable, all susceptible to weakness and temptation. Accountability to our Christian peers serves as a check of our inbred tendency to folly. See how to link-up with other Christians and become accountable at the end of the chapter.

Put Out the Fire

The devil flings his flaming arrows from near and far. None strike nearer than the passionate temptations, or those that spring from our tendency to lust. The most common word used in the New Testament for lust is *epithumia*, defined as "an active desire springing from a diseased soul."[4]

Consider the following Scripture references:

"But I say to you that whoever looks at a woman to lust for her has already committed adultery with her in his heart." (Matthew 5:28)

"Now these things became our examples, to the intent that we should not lust after evil things as they also lusted." (1 Corinthians 10:6)

"I say then: Walk in the Spirit, and you shall not fulfill the *lust* of the flesh. For the flesh lusts against the Spirit, and the Spirit against the flesh; and these are contrary to one another, so that you do not do the things that you wish." (Galatians 5:16)

"Let no one say when he is tempted, 'I am tempted by God; for God cannot be tempted by evil nor does He Himself tempt anyone. But each one is tempted when he is drawn away by his own desires and enticed. Then, when desire has conceived, it gives birth to sin; and sin, when it is full-grown, brings forth death." (James 1:13-15)

The saving blood of Jesus Christ has healed our sin-diseased souls, but there remains a tendency within us to give in to carnal impulses. Arrows flung near and far fly in disguises. What, for instance, does sex appeal have to do with selling a car or a meal? Everything. The makers of cars and meals know that humans are interested in and titillated by pretty things. They shoot their arrows out at random, hoping to penetrate the soft skin of unguarded targets.

The importance of the Breastplate in exercising self-control over our natural impulses and turning back the slings and arrows cannot be overstated. Without it, the arrows are as guided missiles aimed squarely at our weaknesses. Satan poisons arrows at the tips with the shame and guilt of past transgressions in order to catalyze, precipitate, and hasten our fall and interrupt our grasping for grace.

A friend of mine recounted that every time he reached a certain level in his Christian growth, he was pulled up short by feelings of guilt and inadequacy. This went on for years before he shared his struggle. A small accountability group assisted him in resolving these feelings.

I had pastored for almost thirty years before realizing the importance and value of small accountability groups. It was long in coming because of my own reluctance to be held personally accountable.

In the course of counseling several men who were each struggling with secret addictions, I admitted my own challenge in holding myself personally accountable for my transgressions. I found it all too easy to cast off responsibility for my actions on others. Church members seemed all too eager to speak of my faults aloud with others. When I shared my weakness with the men, their response both surprised and strengthened me. While the words they spoke were difficult to hear, when I reflected on them, I apprehended both their wisdom and sincerity. It was just what I needed.

We formed a group, by accident, meeting irregularly at first, then regularly. We linked up our Shields of Accountability and became accountable to each other. Through the truth and sincerity we spoke to each other, we learned to be more accountable to ourselves. We fight a shared battle with our Shields linked up against the enemies *without* and *within*. We founded, at least in our little circle, a way to quench the fires within. If not for my foolish pride, I would have recognized earlier the value of small accountability groups.

A small accountability group can function using the acronym C. A. R. T.

"C" is for Confession. James wrote in his Epistle to "Confess your trespasses to one another, and pray for one another, that you may be healed." (James 5:16)

"A" is for Accountability. When we allow others to question us honestly, the simplicity and directness of their questions may shock us out of our zone of comfort.

"Are you still a man of God?"

"Still a man of God? I've been a pastor for thirty years, and you ask whether I am a man of God?" It is an honest question begging an honest answer.

Once we promised to pray with our wives on a daily basis. Over dinner one evening, one of my brothers asked my wife, in my presence, if I had been praying with her daily. Rather than become offended, I admired his concern for my spiritual development, his "checking up" on me.

"R" is for Responsibility. We "Bear one another's burdens and so fulfill the law of Christ." (Galatians 6:2)

"T" is for Transparency. None of us is vague or obtuse. We speak our minds without fear of rejection or exposure. By linking our Shields, we deny the enemy entrance among us.

Conclusion

Do you have someone in your life, who holds you accountable? When you find yourself under attack, you need someone with whom you can *link up* in prayer and confession. Learn more about an Armor-bearer in Appendix C.

HOW TO "LINK-UP" SHIELDS IN ACCOUNTABILITY

Philippians 1:27 —

"_____

_____."

To stand firmly with another, we must be unified in spirit, mind and purpose.

Colossians 4:12 —

"_____

_____."

None of us stands alone. We need each other. Linking up Shields is hard work. "Laboring fervently" means "to take pains, to wrestle as in a prize contest, straining every nerve to the uttermost towards the goal."[1]

2 Corinthians 1:21, NLT—

"_____

_____."

No one stands alone for Christ.

1 Thessalonians 3:8—

"_____

_____."

When we are solid in our footing, we encourage others to stand strong.

As you begin your day, memorize and quote one or more of these Scriptures to yourself. Pray for those who are counting on your support. Ask God to send Armor-bearers who can support you. Ask God to teach you to be an Armor-bearer.

Chapter Five

The Helmet of Salvation

With the Helmet, we proclaim both *who* we are and *whose* we are. The Helmet does not protect the mind. The heart is the source of thoughts, and it is guarded by the Breastplate.

Who Are We?

The Helmet marks us as Christians. It's a means of telling friend from foe. Even in the same army, different helmets or crests distinguish units.

It is the Helmet of *Salvation*. It does not simply mean that we are saved. We are also in the company of *the saved*.

Wearing the Helmet demonstrates to the enemy where our loyalties lie. It is a signal that there is no compromise.

Wearing the Helmet buttresses and reaffirms our fellow Christians, who like all humans are from time to time fallow and unpredictable. But finding other Christians to bolster us, as Isaiah wrote (Isaiah 59:19), we are as the Spirit of God moving a battle flag, a rallying point in times of vulnerability. That is why the Helmet is worn high on the head, so that it may be seen. When the enemy threatens, Christians rally round the standard lifted up on high.

It is like trumpeting in our ears, a drumbeat, our hearts, pounding in our chests. "Wherever you hear the sound of the trumpet, rally to us there. Our God will fight for us," wrote Nehemiah (Nehemiah 4:20). The Holy Spirit moves us to minister to our brothers and sisters in need. But we cannot know them all, and many we don't know need us, are heartened when they see us standing tall, wearing our Helmets proudly. The seeds we sow in the world unwittingly are riches. The manner in which we spread them manifests to whom the bounty goes that we shall sacrifice, ourselves to Almighty God.

The Helmet is the crowning of the Christian soldier.

Whose Are We?

The Helmet also identifies *whose* we are. The Helmet gives us shelter from arrows shot at our heads, but it also is a reminder, by its own weight of who we are. We are soldiers and among us is a chain-of-command.

When Jesus entered into Capernaum in Luke 7, a Centurion sent for him to come and heal his sick servant. But when Jesus came near, the Centurion sent his friends saying he thought himself not worthy to have Jesus under his roof, "but say the word," the Centurion said, "and my servant will be healed."

Then the Centurion, a man of military rank, compared his post with that of Jesus. "For I also am a man placed under authority, having soldiers under me. And I say to one, 'Go,' and he goes; and to another, 'Come,' and he comes; and to my servant, 'Do this,' and he does it."

When his servants sought out Jesus, they told him the Centurion was worthy of having his servant healed, for they said, "He loves our nation, and he has built us a synagogue." The Centurion, despite his allegiance to Rome, had extended what David had established in Judah, when God through the prophet Nathan in 2 Samuel 7:7 commanded, "Why build ye not a house of cedar?"

An exasperated David prays to God in Verse 19: "And yet this was a small thing in Your sight, O Lord God; but You have also spoken of Your servant's house for a great while to come. Is this the manner of man, O Lord God?"

By the house David established, the Word and the Kingdom of God were made real on Earth, "And your house and your kingdom shall be established forever before you. Your throne shall be established forever," God said.

Twenty-eight generations later, Jesus stood marveling at the Centurion, who believed his servant would be healed. Though a man of rank, he submitted to Jesus. Jesus "turned around and said to the crowd that followed Him, 'I say to you, I have not found such great faith, not even in Israel.' And those who were sent, returning to the house, found the servant well who had been sick." (Luke 7:8-10)

While as humans, we may exalt in our lordship, as Christians, we must learn the fine art of submission. The Greek word for *submission*, hupotasso, is a military term meaning "to arrange under, to subordinate, put in subjec-tion."[1] A form of the word is used in each of the following Scriptures:

"Because the carnal mind is enmity against God; for it is not subject to the law of God, nor indeed can be." (Romans 8:7)

"Therefore you must be subject, not only because of wrath but also for conscience' sake." (Romans 13:5)

"Let your women .... Be submissive, as the law also says." (1 Corinthians 14:34)

"Wives, submit to your own husbands, as is fitting in the Lord." (Colossians 3:18)

"Remind them to be subject to rulers and authorities, to obey, to be ready for every good work." (Titus 3:1)

"Servants, be submissive to your masters with all fear, not only to the good and gentle, but also to the harsh." (1 Peter 2:18)

Our wisdom should not displace that of our master's. The foremost lesson of boot camp is to train soldiers to obey their superiors. There isn't time in the heat of battle to explain orders. They must be carried out.

To fail to come under submission is to rebel or be insubordinate. As Samuel tells a recalcitrant King Saul in the Book of Samuel, "Hath the Lord as great delight in burnt offerings and sacrifices, as in obeying the voice of the Lord? Behold, to obey is better than sacrifice, and to hearken than the fat of rams. For rebellion is as the sin of witchcraft, and stubbornness is as iniquity and idolatry." (1 Samuel 15:22-23, KJV)

Every human, Christian or otherwise, is placed by God under the authority of parents, under government, under employers and pastors and other masters. To launch forth into spiritual conflict full of stubbornness and iniquity is to invite defeat. As soon as we take off the protective covering of the Helmet, the devil sets us in his sights. God cannot protect us in battle which is the product of sin and rebellion.

Are you under authority? Have you obeyed your parents' instruction? Are you under the covering and protection of your church and pastor? Do you regularly regard legal requirements, such as speed laws? Obey the laws and obey your parents, which are just. Obey the just church and a just pastor. Do not do as King Saul and ignore the word of direction from God's prophet. When King Saul abandoned

Samuel, he took off his Helmet and sought God's will through a witch. When he put on the Helmet as the first king of Israel, it would not fit. His head was too big.

We can shrink our heads down to size, be humble before God and those He placed in authority in our lives, and avoid the fate to which Saul was sentenced for his transgressions and failure to surrender his will. Peter said, "Likewise, you younger people, submit yourselves to your elders. Yes, all of you be submissive to one another, and be clothed with humility, for God resists the proud, but gives grace to the humble. Therefore humble yourselves under the mighty hand of God, that He may exalt you in due time." (1 Peter 5:5, 6)

Conclusion

Make a list of people you have rejected based on your desire to be free of their expectations. Ask God for guidance and confirmation. Speak with them, humble yourself. Ask forgiveness and seek to come back under their authority, if they are just. When you reconcile with your just masters, the Helmet will fit snugly on your head. Through it, God will pour His grace in and through you.

When you wear the Helmet, you declare yourself a child of God. Be worthy of the honor.

HOW TO "PUT ON" THE
HELMET OF SALVATION

The Helmet identifies *who* we are and *whose* we are. We stand with our feet firmly planted and heads held high, with the assurance that we are impregnable when the Armor of God shields us.

Memorize these Scriptures and rehearse them aloud, especially when you feel rebellious or alone.

1 Corinthians 16:13 —

"_____

_____."

Who we are is who God says we are. We may feel weak and afraid, but God says we are strong and brave. Wearing the Helmet of Salvation enables us to "stand fast in the faith."

1 Thessalonians 3: 8 —

"_____

_____."

To know *whose* we are is also to acknowledge our brother and sister Christians, some who wear the Helmet and others who struggle to make it fit. Our interdependence marks us. Christians and non-Christians alike are encouraged by our example. Our brothers and sisters are counting on us for support.

Chapter Six

The Sword of the Spirit

N ow with the Sword of the Spirit we slice our way forward. There is no retreat. Time moves us onward. Whether we progress to become the people God wants us to be or whether we are cast adrift on waves, floating wherever the current takes us, is our choice.

When we stray from the forward path, when we turn aside—turn away, our backsides are exposed. There is no Armor there. We mustn't expose ourselves. Our unending offensive is our best defense, and the offense depends on our wielding the Sword of the Spirit.

Take Up the Sword

Two words are used for "sword" in the New Testament. The first word is *rhomphaia,* which refers to a large Thracian sword.[1] The Thracian sword resembles the broadsword of the Middle Ages and is the sword of judgment referred to several times in the Book of Revelation. (Revelation 1:16; 2:12, 16; 19:15, 21)

The second word is *machaira,* a short sword or a dagger.[2] Roman soldiers used this sword in close, hand-to-hand combat. This is the Sword of our test.

When flaming arrows flung from afar bounce off our Breastplate, our Shield, and our Helmet, Satan and his minions give them up for knives. They walk among us disguised as friends, waiting to press them in our backs. They are all around us, armed, waiting for us to take off our Armor. When they grow weary of waiting, they strike from the front with vicious but poorly-executed strokes. The dagger's diminutive size and lightness enables us to turn swinging and striking with the Sword in rapid thrusts, deflecting strokes aimed at us while executing offensive slashes and thrusts.

The Defensive Sword

In the only recorded occasion of personal conflict with Satan, in Matthew 4:1-11, Jesus uses the Word of God defensively.

"Then Jesus was led up by the Spirit into the wilderness to be tempted by the devil," Matthew writes. "And when He had fasted forty days and forty nights, afterward He was hungry. Now then the tempter came to Him, he said, 'If you are the Son of God, command that these stones become bread.'"

But Jesus replied, "It is written, Man shall not live by bread alone, but by every word that proceeds from the mouth of God."

Satan preyed on Jesus' hunger and tempted him to "command stones to become bread." Jesus countered, quoting a passage from Deuteronomy 8:3 (KJV), declaring the priority of the Word of God above all, even life-sustaining nutrition: "Man shall not live by bread alone, but by every word that proceedeth out of the mouth of God."

"Then the devil," Matthew wrote, took Jesus "up into the holy city, set Him on the pinnacle of the temple," and said: "If You are the Son of God, throw Yourself down, For it is written: 'He shall give His angels charge over you. In their hands they shall bear you up, lest you dash your foot against a stone.'"

Then Jesus said, "It is written again, You shall not tempt the Lord your God."

Satan challenged the authenticity of the Word of God, quoting Psalm 91:11, 12, exhorting Jesus to throw Himself down, for it was written that the angels, who had charge over Him, would deliver Him, or "bear Him up." Why fast in the desert forty days and forty nights? Why endure temptation? Why not fall and let God's angels lift Him up?

The devil had the presumption to test God rather than trust Him. God tests us just as He allowed the devil to test Jesus. We are to trust Him, not tempt Him. "You shall not tempt the Lord your God." (Deuteronomy 6:16)

The devil took Jesus "up on an exceedingly high mountain and showed Him all the kingdoms of the world and their glory. He said to Jesus, 'All these things I will give You if You will fall down and worship me.'"

Jesus said, "Away with you, Satan! For it is written, 'You shall worship the Lord your God, and Him only you shall serve.'" The devil left Him, and the angels came and ministered to Him.

The devil valued form over substance, the idea of service over worship, as if it did not matter who Jesus served as long as he served someone. The devil's cynicism is not unlike our own, prone to accommodation of subjective truth and a humanistic inclusiveness that negotiates fundamental values and beliefs at the core of Christianity.

Jesus commands Satan in Matthew 4:10 (KJV), quoting Deuteronomy 6:13: "Get thee hence, Satan: for it is written, Thou shalt worship the Lord thy God, and Him only shalt thou serve."

The Word of God must be kept close at hand to rebuff Satan. David spoke of hiding God's Word in his heart, "That I might not sin against You." (Psalm 119:11) Using the weapon is a learned art. While we are to "take up" the Sword of the Spirit as needed, we will not know what to do with it if we do not learn how to use it. We must practice using it. We do so by learning and studying the Word of God.

TRAINING IN THE WORD OF GOD

The Greek New Testament employs primarily two terms for the Word of God. They are *logos* and *rhema*. Vine's Expository Dictionary makes the following distinction between the two words:

"The significance of rhema ... is exemplified in the injunction to take 'the Sword of the Spirit, which is the Word [rhema] of God.'" (Ephesians 6:17) Here, the reference is not to the whole Bible as such, but to the individual Scripture which the Spirit brings to our remembrance for use in time of need, a prerequisite being the regular storing of the mind with Scripture [logos]. [3]

Logos refers to the total written Word of God. Without the logos of God's Word, there can be no rhemas. John wrote in 1:1 that "In the beginning was the Word [logos], and the Word [logos] was with God, and the Word [logos] was God."

The narrower term, rhema, is more specific, referring to the literal, anointed Word from God for us. The Spirit brings the Word, rhema, to us, in defense, depending on the nature of the attack.

In Hebrews 4:12, the Apostle Paul writes, "For the Word [rhema] of God is living and powerful, and sharper than any two-edged sword, piercing even to the division of soul and spirit, and of joints and marrow, and is a discerner of the thoughts and intents of the heart." The Sword we "take up" is a living thing. Jesus expresses as much in Matthew 10:19-20: "But when they deliver you up, do not worry about how or what you should speak, for it will be given to you in that hour what you should speak; for it is not you who speak, but the Spirit of your Father who speaks in you."

God will give you the right word at the right time to speak in your own defense. The rhema Word of God is a powerful tool to deflect the attacks of Satan and his hordes.

Memorize the following Scriptures that allow us to "unsheathe" the Sword:

2 Thessalonians 2:15—

"_____

_____."

This is a rhema Word.

2 Thessalonians 2:16, 17—

"_____

_____."

This is a rhema Word.

2 Corinthians 6:4-7—

"_____

_____."

This is a rhema Word.

Chapter Seven

The Christian Soldier's Weapon – Prayer

Each piece of the Armor of God is issued for the defense of the Christian. Even the Sword of the Spirit, the only offensive weapon in the catalog of Armor, is to be used primarily in defense.

The only truly offensive weapon Christians possess— but also the most powerful—is prayer. In his letter to the Ephesians, Paul exhorts his brethren to pray "always with all prayer and supplication in the Spirit, being watchful to this end with all perseverance and supplication for all the saints." (Ephesians 6:18)

With the Armor adorning us, we are impregnable. When protected Christians wield the weapon of prayer, it sends the devil and his hordes scattering. The devil is not afraid of the Word of God. He knows it by heart. But he uses it cynically to confound the children of God and sow doubt in their hearts.

The following five forms of prayer are those that strengthen and reaffirm our Christian character. Like our Helmets, they identify us, metaphysically, as of and belonging to the Holy Spirit.

1. *Adoration or Praise.* Christians are "To speak in praise of God"[1] as the Apostles model in Acts 2:46-47 and 3:8, 9. Earlier, St. Luke writes at 19:37, "Then, as [Jesus] was now drawing near the descent of the Mount of Olives, the whole multitude of the disciples began to rejoice and *praise* God with a loud voice for all the mighty works they had seen."

2. *Thanksgiving.* Believers are encouraged to abound in joy for the fruitfulness and bounty of creation.[2] In Colossians

2:6,7 Paul writes, "As you therefore have received Christ Jesus the Lord, so walk in Him, rooted and built up in Him and established in the faith, as you have been taught, *abounding in it with thanksgiving*." Paul writes again of thanksgiving in 2 Corinthians 4:15: "For all things are for your sakes, that grace, having spread through the many, may cause *thanksgiving to abound* to the glory of God." In 2 Corinthians 9:12, he writes again: "For the administration of this service not only supplies the needs of the saints, but also is *abounding* through many *thanksgivings* to God."

3. *Confession*. Confession is the prayer of a sinner that God has committed to hear. The word is a compound verb meaning, "to speak the same thing,"[3] or to agree with God about personal guilt. St. John wonderfully expresses the idea in 1 John 1:9: "If we *confess* our sins, He is faithful and just to forgive us our sins and to cleanse us from all unrighteousness."

The Apostle Paul uses the same term in Romans 10:9, 10: "If you *confess* with your mouth the Lord Jesus and believe in your heart that God has raised Him from the dead, you will be saved. For with the heart one believes unto righteousness, and with the mouth *confession* is made unto salvation." This prayer is so important, Paul says, that we cannot be saved without it.

4. *Petition.* The Lord stands ready to hear the needs of His people: "For the eyes of the Lord are on the righteous, and His ears are open to their prayers; but the face of the Lord is against those who do evil." (1 Peter 3:12) The Lord is as eager to hear our petitions as we are to receive answers, as long as our petitions are just.

5. *Supplication.* Supplication is similar to intercession. Paul writes of "Praying always with all prayer and *supplication* in the Spirit ... with all perseverance and *supplication* for all the saints." (Ephesians 6:18) Jesus interceded on Peter's behalf, as reported in Luke 22:31-32, telling him, "Simon, Simon! Indeed, Satan has asked for you, that he may sift you as wheat. But *I have prayed for you*, that your faith should not fail, and when you have returned to Me, strengthen your brethren." Jesus interceded for Peter and, through His prayer on Peter's behalf, was confident of a positive outcome.

Warfare Prayer

It is the intercessor's prayer of supplication that is the prayer of spiritual warfare. It was the prayer Jesus offered in Luke 22:44 in the Garden of Gethsemane—"And being in agony, He prayed more earnestly." *Agonia*, translated as agony, refers to "combat, contest, giving prominence to the pain and labor of the conflict."[4] Paul writes in Colossians 4:12-13 of the intercessor Epaphras. "Epaphras, who is one of you, a bondservant of Christ, greets you, always laboring fervently [agonizomai] for you in prayers, that you may stand perfect and complete in all the will of God."

Epaphras is a spiritual leader to be singled out among many, in Paul's eyes, because he is a man of prayer, a man for whom Paul begged, in Romans 15:30, writing: "Now I beg you, brethren, through the Lord Jesus Christ, and through the love of the Spirit, that you strive together [sunagonizomai] with me in prayers to God for me." Paul sought prayers of intercession as a covering over his person, as an Armor to hold up as a Shield against the enemy's onslaught as he fought on the frontlines in spiritual warfare.

In the same manner, the early Church interceded on behalf of Peter. When Peter was imprisoned after James' murder, after Herod saw how the murder "pleased the

Jews," and planned to bring Peter forth before the people after Easter, much as Jesus had been brought forth, with presumably the same end in mind, "prayer was made without ceasing of the church unto God for him." An angel came and freed him. Peter walked to the house "where many were gathered together praying," and knocked at the door. Rhoda, who answered the door, and the others within, when they saw Peter, were so shocked they thought they saw his angel. They were *astonished* at the results of their warfare prayer.

Do you wonder how many others like Peter we could free from spiritual prison if we gathered in prayer to pull down the devil's strongholds as in Acts 12:1-17?

James writes in 5:16-18 that "The effective, fervent prayer of a righteous man avails much. Elijah was a man with a nature like ours, and he prayed earnestly that it would not rain; and it did not rain on the land for three years and six months. And he prayed again, and the heaven gave rain, and the earth produced its fruit."

Warfare prayer can turn the tide in spiritual battles. We never should discount the power of prayer or relegate it to the last resort, because it is the only means by which Christians may engage the enemy in spiritual warfare. It is, with the limited exception of the Sword, our only offensive weapon.

Our preaching, our singing, our teaching and our Christian worship services are useless and, perhaps, futile if they do not feature prayer. Only by prayer—intercessory prayer—can we enter the realm of the Spirit and take on the devil and his hordes. Without it, we are fooling ourselves.

Satan and his hordes are interlopers who know well the terrain of God's territory. They use and abuse God's Church for their own selfish purposes. The Church is charged to sort out the interlopers and not only stand firm against them, but to press our spiritual advantage. Protected by God's Armor, intercessory prayer allows us to advance into the enemy's strongholds and pull them down, as we take the initiative mentioned in 2 Corinthians 10:4-5.

Sheltered by the Armor of God, we establish a foothold in enemy territory, launching sorties and raids that force the enemy to retreat. While we engage the enemy on the field of spiritual battle, the power of intercessory prayer spoken by us and for us engages the enemy from above and from within. Even when we are far from the frontlines, we can provide support through agonizing warfare praying.

In order to establish a foothold, or "firebase," we must:

1. Conduct reconnaissance patrols. Select a worthwhile target for intercession and recruit several Christians to unite in prayer. Often persons who irritate us most in life as a result of their own unhappiness and dissatisfaction are most in need of prayer.

2. Develop accountability with prayer partners. Conduct an Armor check. Make sure prayer group members are dressed for battle. The enemy will seek out any weakness in any individual in the group and use it to sow dissension and distrust.

3. Send up a general prayer covering as well as prayers of intercession for specific individuals. Pray aggressively for the success of their missions.

4. Gain ground by converting the lost. Those held captive by Satan are not without personal choice, but when the spells of Satan are broken by fervent prayers of intercession, it makes it possible for sinners to turn away from the past. Our presence in opposition to the enemy's intentions to destroy our world is vital. We must take ownership for the part of the world within our reach, or else risk losing it.

5. Consolidate our position. We can't stop at winning the lost. We must gather them into a good church family and train them to wear the Armor of God. We must have faith, as Jesus did, that they, like Peter, will venture out into harm's way, as "fishers of men," to win the lost to the light of Jesus Christ. Our multitudinous prayers of covering are as the upturned Shield of Faith, sheltering our expanding Kingdom of God from Satan and his hordes.

Satan knows well the Word of God, but he twists and distorts it to deceive the very people who seek to know it. When intercessory prayer is coupled with the sharp Sword of God's Word, demons melt away before the light of God's absolute truth. The Word is an awesome weapon when handled by Spirit-filled soldiers who have learned to gain victory through prayer. Scripture promises believers ultimate victory and predicts the downfall of all who oppose truth. "No weapon formed against you shall prosper, and every tongue which rises against you in judgment you shall condemn. This is the heritage of the servants of the Lord and their righteousness is from Me, says the Lord." (Isaiah 54:17)

WARFARE STRATEGIES

Human history bears witness to the rise and fall of vast empires, empires that invariably featured strong military forces that established and maintained nation-states under the banners of various religions and ideologies.

During the time of Christ and centuries prior, human warfare was relatively simple. Armies either met on the field of battle in hand-to-hand combat or an invading force laid siege to fortified cities and towns. Oftentimes the besieged hid behind moats or walled fortresses, allowing invaders to pillage the countryside in search of provisions.

For far too long, the Church body has hidden behind its own walls, surrendering the countryside to the devil and his hordes. The peek-a-boo Christians of modernity are a sad shadow of our Christian forbearers, who embarked on near-mythic missions that featured dangers from all sides, "enemies compassed about," near-certain defeat, and certain death. While much could be achieved by a unified thrust on enemy soil, such an offensive seems unlikely from an increasingly fragmented Christian Church. The sad epilogue to the Christian story is, as it is written, we have surrendered the vast countryside to an invading force.

What would Jesus say of our strategy of warfare?
Matthew 28:19—

"_____

_____."

Jesus said to "Go," not come. His strategy was infiltration, not invitation.

Jesus commanded. Mark 16:15—

"_____

_____."

Jesus did not say to advertise in order to draw a crowd, He said to "Go" where the people are and preach the Gospel to them.

Paul boldly declared to the unbelieving Jews of Antioch in Pisidia. Acts 13:14, 16—

"_____

_____."

Isaiah prophesied about the Lord's Kingdom in Isaiah 9:7—

"_____

_____."

The world has not yet witnessed the far-flung Kingdom of God described in Isaiah. Will we be the ones to see it, and will we be the ones to build it? If so, we have our work cut out for us.

Before we begin to build it and before we embark on our own epic quest, we must learn to wear the Armor of God. We must learn to keep it on even in the heat of battle, even when it chafes and burns and we want nothing more than to free ourselves of the weight of the Armor.

We must first become the children God designed us to be, then we can embark on a quest to "Go and make disciples of all the nations, baptizing them in the name of the Father and of the Son and of the Holy Spirit, teaching them to observe all things that I have commanded you; and I am with you always, even to the end of the age." (Matthew 28:18-20)

CONCLUSION

A las, we Christians are armed to the hilt with the Armor of God. *"Gird Your sword upon Your thigh, O Mighty One, with Your glory and Your majesty. And in Your majesty, ride prosperously because of truth, humility and righteousness; and Your right hand shall teach You awesome things. Our arrows are sharp in the heart of the King's enemies; the peoples fall under You."* (Psalm 45:3-5)

"Gird your sword upon Your thigh, O Mighty One."
We wield the Sword of the Spirit. By it we strike out into the heart of darkness with the light of God's Word.

"And in your <u>majesty</u> ride prosperously."

Ride tall and firm with your head held high, bearing the Helmet of Salvation.

"Ride prosperously because of <u>truth</u>."

Prosperously means to "break through; be successful."[1] Wear the Belt of Truth, a symbol of your favor and advertisement of your trust.

"Ride prosperously because of ...<u>humility</u>."

When warriors humbly wear the Shoes of Peace, we gain the favor of God. *"God resists the proud, but gives grace to the humble."* (James 4:6)

"Ride prosperously because of ... <u>righteousness</u>."
Wear proudly the Breastplate of Righteousness, an outward symbol of His righteousness in us.

And your right hand shall teach You awesome things."
Our mighty and prosperous King is our shield-mate. We faithfully guard His right and His left. We share in the work of His powerful hands, bearing up in our hands the Shield of Faith.

Put on the Armor of God

Stand tall and let your Helmet of Salvation be seen. You are proud to be identified with Him and His cause.

As you settle the Breastplate of Righteousness in place, honor yourself by your thoughts and your King by your words. *Shape up* what you think and how you feel.

107

When you *cinch up* the Belt of Truth, cinch it tight, even if the truth hurts.

Lace up the Shoes of the preparation of the Gospel of Peace by rehearsing the Word of God. Don't just read the Bible; seek out the principles that underlay the text and apply them in your life.

Take up the Sword of the Spirit in anticipation of the battles which are sure to come your way. Practice at spiritual combat by quoting the Scriptures aloud.

Link up Shields of Faith with fellow Christians and rebuff the slings and arrows cast from near and far. We bolster and guide each other in times of weakness. Isolated, we can be vulnerable. Together, we are invincible.

Stand for inspection using the following memory aid:

Always

> Belt: *cinch up*
>
> Breastplate: *shape up*
>
> Shoes: *lace up*

As needed

> Shield: *hook up*
>
> Helmet: *wear proudly*
>
> Sword: *take up*

CODA

We are in a war, like it or not. We are called to resist the enemy, to strike out against his hordes and force their retreat from us. We must make a stand. We can be invincible if we equip ourselves with God's Armor.

We cannot grow complacent, comfortable on our beachhead. We are building an eternal kingdom, not a temporary fort.

We are deceived when we think we exist merely to enjoy life and lay up treasures for our time on Earth. The things of this life are good, and there is a place for them, but our first purpose on Earth is to establish the Kingdom of God.

Engaging the enemy in spiritual combat may impinge on our desire for the comforts of this world, but we must be ever mindful that we are in a war, lest the enemy deceive us into sinful accommodation. We may hide our heads in the sand, but the war still rages for the soul of mankind on the shores of our sheltered existence.

Unless and until we understand this and prepare for battle, we are in no position to oppose the devil.

Wearing every piece of the Armor of God is essential to withstand the devil's attacks. Forgetting, dismantling, choosing not to wear but one piece renders us vulnerable to the shards and stones and flaming arrows of his hordes.

We must burnish ourselves with God's Armor, stand firm and let our Helmets of Salvation and our Breastplates of Righteousness be seen. We are the righteous ones. We are the ones to chase the devil away.

We are the ones to leave the fort, to travel inland into the heart of darkness, to set the captives free, pull down enemy strongholds and establish the Kingdom of God forever.

APPENDICES

LESSONS FOR ADVANCED STUDIES

Appendix A

FASTING

"Fasting is a primary means of spiritual restoration. Fasting releases us from the bondage of our own fleshly desires, allowing the Holy Spirit to revive us spiritually. Fasting moves us deeper into the Christ-like life we were born to live and endows us with a greater awareness of God's reality and presence in our lives.

- Fasting purifies us spiritually.
- Fasting increases our spiritual perception by quieting our minds and emotions.
- Fasting wrings in us a yielding nature, a holy brokenness, an inner calm and self-control.
- Fasting renews our spiritual vision.

- Fasting inspires determination to follow God's revealed plan for our life."[1]

A fast may be partial or absolute.

Consider the following examples of an absolute (complete) fast:

Esther 4:16—

"_____

_____."

Deuteronomy 9:9—

"_____

_____."

Ezra 10:6—

"_____

_____."

Consider an example of a partial fast (abstinence from certain foods only), also known as a "Daniel Fast":

Daniel 10:3—

"_____
_____
_____."

When should we fast?

When interceding for others, as in:

Ezra 10:6—

"_____
_____
_____."

Deuteronomy 9:8-9—

"_____
_____
_____."

I Samuel 20:34—

"_____
_____
_____."

When humbling ourselves, as in:

Psalm 69:10—

"_____
_____
_____."

When seeking God's direction, as in:

Ezra 8:21—

"_____

_____."

Judges 20:26-28—

"_____

_____."

2 Chronicles 20:3, 4—

"_____

_____."

Acts 13:2, 3—

"_____

_____."

When in need of healing, as in:

Isaiah 58:6, 8—

"_____

_____."

Acts 9:9—

"_____

_____."

When in need of deliverance, as in:

Matthew 17:17-20, 21—

"_____

_____."

Appendix B

BOOT CAMP PRIORITIES

M any new converts enjoy a brief grace period before the need arises to engage in spiritual warfare. It seems the devil is held at bay while young Christians learn to wear the Armor of God. Peter suggests as much when he describes a new believer's progress toward spiritual maturity in 2 Peter 1:5-8:

"

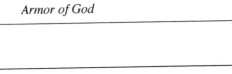

."

The key word is "add." It is translated from the Greek word *epichoregeo* and is understood as *chorus*. It means "to supply in copious measure, to provide beyond the need, to supply more than generously."[1] Each stage is dependent upon the previous stage and flows into the succeeding one. From faith to virtue, to knowledge, to self-control, "boot-camp" is a time of preparation, perseverance, and testing.

The foremost priorities in boot camp are:

Faith

This word is translated from the Greek *pistis* and is not so much an act as a state of being.[2] It refers to a new-found faith in Jesus Christ. It also represents a change of identity. The recruit has become a soldier, and that status distinguishes one from the rest of mankind. Likewise, "Therefore, if anyone is in Christ, he is a new creation; old things have passed away; behold, all things have become new." (2 Corinthians 5:17) The step of faith is life changing.

Virtue

Virtue is a kind of "moral energy"[3] or Godly enthusiasm, resulting from a new-found faith in Christ. Can you remember the excitement when you were first saved, when you came to know Jesus as your Savior? If you were like me, you had a "zeal, but not according to knowledge." (Romans 10:2) I had much to learn, but the nervous energy of newness can be put to good use: studying and memorizing Scripture.

Knowledge

Boot camp is nothing without manuals to study, classes to attend, weapons to assemble and disassemble, barracks to straighten, uniforms to press and countless other tasks to learn and perfect. Days are endless blurs of activity. In the evenings, in quiet time alone, there is no substitute for the study and memorization of God's Word in the life of the newborn Christian. The Psalmist expressed as much in Psalm 119:11-16:

"_____

_____

_____

_____

_____."

Self-Control

Self-control is exercised when we learn "To hold the passions and desires in hand."[4] Self-control is possible when we have gained knowledge of God's expectations for us as revealed in His Word. Self-control prevents us from bolting when the pressure is great. It allows us to stand firm under fire.

Appendix C

BE AN ARMOR-BEARER

R ead and meditate on 1 Samuel 14:1-14.

Every true leader needs Armor-bearers—leaders like Jonathan who are:

Restless. Armor-bearers of true leaders who are not content with the status quo, as was King Saul and his army, who lay vulnerable to their enemies while resting under a shade tree.

Reliable. Armor-bearers as Jonathan, who knew God (1 Samuel 14:6). He could be counted on to apply God's principles. (1Samuel 14:6)

Risk-taker. Armor-bearers of true leaders with faith that God will show them the way of success. (1 Samuel 14:8-10)

Relentless. Armor-bearers of great leaders do not quit until the task is finished.

Great leaders need great Armor-bearers like Jonathan's, who are:

Humble. A man's name is not given. (1 Samuel 14:1. He is fulfilled in serving another.

Faithful. He hears God through a leader he trusts and is willing to risk his own life.

Strong. An Armor-bearer does heavy lifting, holding up the leader to God with prayers of intercession.

Sensitive, with faith. An Armor-bearer is alert to danger. (1 Samuel 14:7)

Dependable. An Armor-bearer guards his leader's back. (1 Samuel 14:12, 13)

Be an Armor-bearer of God.

Appendix D

OVERCOMING DISCOURAGEMENT

A ll Christians become discouraged. It is one of the scourges of our fallen nature and walks hand-in-hand with doubt. Signals of discouragement include:

- Poor appetite, weight loss, or excessive eating with accompanying weight gain;
- Inability to sleep, or excessive sleep;
- Hyperactivity, or listlessness;
- Loss of energy, fatigue;
- Feelings of worthlessness;
- Inability to concentrate;
- Recurring thoughts of suicide.

We must learn to overcome discouragement and self-doubt before we can confront the enemy.

How to Remedy Discouragement:

✓ Remove Guilt:

I John 1:8, 9—

"_____

_____."

✓ Pray alone to God:

Luke 6:12—

"_____

_____."

✓ Distance yourself from fearmongers:

Deuteronomy 20:8—

"_____

_____."

✓ Focus on God's reputation, not on personal shortcomings:

Matthew 6:9—

"_____

_____."

✓ Offer to God a sacrifice of praise:

I Thessalonians 5:18—

"_____

_____."

Appendix E

DEFENSIVE CHESS
STRATEGIES

Chess is said to have been invented by an Indian philosopher in the Sixth Century. Originally called Chaturanga, the game soon spread to Persia, where it was from the Persian word *Shahmat* that the word "chess" was derived.

Chess is a military game in which the goal was and still is to trap the King. To win at Chess, a player must learn not only to capture enemy pieces but also to defend one's own pieces.

Like pieces on a Chess board, we cannot be successful at capturing the enemy if we are not protected. As Christians, we are protected by the Armor of God.

Consider a few Chess strategies that we as Christians can utilize metaphorically:

1. *Pawns are not expendable.* An amateur will sacrifice pawns to clear the way for the big guns from the King's row. But once a piece is swept from the board, it can't return. Not only does that hurt the overall defense, the pawn is the only piece on the board with unlimited potential. That is because the pawn can become anything once it reaches the eighth rank on the board.

   In church ministry, the pawn is the laity, or non-clergy. The main purpose of the Church is to equip the saints *"for the work of ministry."* (Ephesians 4:12, emphasis added) The laity should be encouraged and equipped for the work of ministry and must be protected in order to reach full potential in Christ.

2. *Pawns protect pawns.* Pawns protect each other from the rear. When a "pawn chain" zigzags across the board, it is a formidable defensive posture. In

fact, the pawn chain is weakest at its base, because it is not guarded by another pawn. Once the base is destroyed, the remaining pawns are weakened. The Scripture provides in Ephesians 5:21:

"_____

_____."

3. *Pawns defend open spaces on the game board.* When properly protected, pawns guard empty spaces from enemy incursions. This resembles the covering power of prayer when we saturate the airwaves prior to a spiritual offensive. Every good work begins with adequate preparation and protection.

Every new believer starts as a pawn. The pawn is protected from a threat by its superiors, the laity by the pastor, the sheep by the shepherd, and so on.

Later, armed with the wisdom gleaned from study and application of God's Word, in daily life, by every word and act, the believer, wearing the Armor of God, strikes out in the darkness with the light of God's Word, pushing the boundaries of His creation outward, onward, forever.

ENDNOTES

Introduction

1 *Warfighting*, United States Marine Corps Staff Noncommissioned Officer Academy, Marine Air- Ground Training and Education Center, Marine Corps Combat Development Command, Quantico, Virginia, page 1-1.

2 Speech, House of Commons, 13 May 1940, in Winston Churchill's *Their Finest Hour*, Boston: Houghton Mifflin, © 1949, page 25.

3 Napoleon Bonaparte.

4 *Wuest's Word Studies from the Greek New Testament*, by Kenneth S. Wuest, Wm. B. Eerdman's Publishing Company, Grand Rapids, Michigan, © 1953, Volume 1, Ephesians and Colossians, Chapter Six, page 141.

5 Ibid, page 142.

6 Ibid, page 142.

7 Ibid, page 141.

8 *The Hebrew-Greek Key Study Bible*, by Spiros Zodhiates, Baker Book House, Grand Rapids, Michigan, © 1984, page 1690.

9 Ibid, page 1705.

10 Ibid, page 1723.

11 *Wuest's Word Studies from the Greek New Testament*, by Kenneth S. Wuest, Wm. B. Eerdman's Publishing Company, Grand Rapids, Michigan, © 1953, Volume 1, Ephesians and Colossians, Chapter Six, page 142.

Chapter One

1 *Vines Expository Dictionary of New Testament Words*, by W. E. Vine, World Bible Publishers, Iowa Falls, Iowa, ©1971, page 241

Chapter Two
[1] *Word Studies in the New Testament*, Volume II, by M.R. Vincent, MacDonald Publishing Company, MacDill AFB, Florida, © 1888, page 867.

Chapter Three
[1] *Word Studies in the New Testament*, Volume II, by M.R. Vincent, MacDonald Publishing Company, MacDill AFB, Florida, © 1888, page 867.

[2] *More of...The Best of Bits & Pieces*, compiled and edited by Rob Gilbert, The Economics Press, Inc. Fairfield, New Jersey, © 1997, page 113, citing Denis Waitley, *Being the Best*, Oliver-Nelson.

[3] *The Best of Bits & Pieces*, compiled and edited by Arthur R. Lenehan, The Economics Press, Inc. Fairfield, New Jersey, © 1994, page 1.

Chapter Four
[1] *Word Studies in the New Testament*, Volume II, by M. R. Vincent, MacDonald Publishing Company, MacDill AFB, Florida, © 1888, page 867.

[2] Ibid, page 867.

[3] Attributed to a Spartan Mother to her son, who was going into battle. It was later picked up by Roman soldiers.

[4] *The Hebrew-Greek Key Study Bible*, by Spiros Zodhiates, Baker Book House, Grand Rapids, Michigan, © 1984, pp 1690, 1717.

How to "Link-Up" Shields in Accountability
[1] *The Hebrew-Greek Key Study Bible*, by Spiros Zodhiates, Baker Book House, Grand Rapids, Michigan, © 1984, page 1658.

Chapter Five
[1] *Wuest's Word Studies From the Greek New Testament*, Volume I, Wm. B. Eerdman's Publishing Company, Grand Rapids, Michigan, © 1953, Ephesians and Colossians, Chapter Five, page 129.

Chapter Six
[1] *Vines Expository Dictionary of New Testament Words*, by W. E. Vine, World Bible Publishers, Iowa Falls, Iowa, ©1971, page 100.

[2] Ibid, page 100.

[3] Ibid, page 230.

Chapter Seven

[1] *Vines Expository Dictionary of New Testament Words*, by W. E. Vine, World Bible Publishers, Iowa Falls, Iowa, ©1971, page 199.

[2] Ibid, page 122.

[3] *The Hebrew-Greek Key Study Bible*, by Spiros Zodhiates, Baker Book House, Grand Rapids, Michigan, © 1984, page 1715.

[4] Ibid, page 1658

Conclusion

[1] *Strong's Exhaustive Concordance of the Bible*, by James Strong, MacDonald Publishing Company, © 1971, page 99 of the Hebrew Bible Dictionary.

Appendix A – Fasting

[1] Adapted from *The Coming Revival: America's Call to Fast, Pray, and Seek God's Face*, Bill Bright, New Life Publications, © 1995.

Appendix B – Boot Camp Priorities

[1] *Wuest's Word Studies From the Greek New Testament*, Volume II, by Kenneth S. Wuest, Wm. B. Eerdman's Publishing Company, Grand Rapids, Michigan, © 1954, 2 Peter, Chapter One, page 23.

[2] *Vines Expository Dictionary of New Testament Words*, by W. E. Vine, World Bible Publishers, Iowa Falls, Iowa, ©1971, page 71.

[3] *Word Studies in the New Testament*, Volume I, by M. R. Vincent, MacDonald Publishing Company, MacDill AFB, Florida, © 1888, page 324.

[4] *Webster's New World College Dictionary*, Fourth Edition, Macmillan, New York, New York, © 1999, page 486.

CPSIA information can be obtained
at www.ICGtesting.com
Printed in the USA
FFOW03n1324120515
13353FF

9 781613 792186